Authentic Leadership: What Really Works

by

Jared L. Scott

Authentic Leadership: What Really Works

by Jared L. Scott

Copyright © 2024 by Jared L. Scott

All rights reserved.

No part of this book may be reproduced, stored in a retrieval system, or transmitted in any form or by any means—electronic, mechanical, photocopying, recording, or otherwise—without the prior written permission of the publisher, except in the case of brief quotations embodied in critical articles and reviews.

ISBN: 9798340444325

Published by: AMAZON

Cover Design and Artwork: Assisted by GPT

First Edition: September 2024

Disclaimer:

This book is a work of non-fiction. The opinions and views expressed in this book are those of the author. The author has made every effort to ensure the accuracy of the information within this book was correct at time of publication. The author does not assume and hereby disclaims any liability to any party for any loss, damage, or disruption caused by errors or omissions, whether such errors or omissions result from negligence, accident, or any other cause.

Acknowledgments

Writing this book has been a journey, one that would not have been possible without the support, guidance, and encouragement of many people.

To my loved ones, thank you for your unwavering support, patience, and understanding throughout this process. Your belief in me and your constant encouragement gave me the strength to see this project through to completion.

I would also like to extend my gratitude to my colleagues and mentors, who have shaped my understanding of leadership over the years. Your insights, feedback, and shared experiences have been invaluable in helping me articulate the concepts and ideas presented in this book.

To the members of my team, both past and present, thank you for your hard work, dedication, and trust. You have taught me as much, if not more, about leadership as I have tried to impart to you. Your willingness to follow me through the ups and downs has made all the difference.

A special thanks to the supportive communities and groups that have been a source of inspiration and reflection. Your collective wisdom and camaraderie have played a significant role in my growth as a leader.

Finally, I want to thank my readers. Your desire to

lead with integrity and purpose is what drives me to share my experiences and insights. I hope that this book provides you with the tools and inspiration to become the leader you aspire to be.

This book is dedicated to all of you. Thank you for being part of my leadership journey.

Foreword

Leadership. It's a word that gets thrown around in every corporate meeting, plastered on motivational posters, and preached in countless seminars. We've all read the books, sat through the PowerPoint presentations, and listened to the buzzwords that promise transformation and success. Yet, despite all the talk, how often do we see real leadership in action? How often do the principles that are so eloquently described actually take root and flourish in the organizations we work for?

The truth is, not often.

Over the years, I've come to realize that for many companies, leadership is more about appearance than action. It's a checkbox on the corporate to-do list, a feel-good exercise that allows executives to pat themselves on the back while the reality on the ground remains unchanged. This book is for those who, like me, have grown cynical of the leadership industry—a multi-billion dollar machine that churns out ideas, but rarely delivers results.

In the pages that follow, I won't just talk about leadership; I'll talk about the leadership that you don't read about in the bestsellers. The kind that isn't glamorous, that doesn't come with easy answers or quick fixes, but is necessary nonetheless. I'll share my experiences—both the successes and the failures—because if there's one thing I've learned, it's that leadership isn't about what you say, it's about what you do.

This book is not for those looking for another set of platitudes. It's for the realists, the skeptics, and the doers who understand that leadership is not a title or a position, but a practice. It's for those who know that talk is cheap, and real leadership requires grit, resilience, and a willingness to confront the uncomfortable truths.

If you've ever felt disillusioned by the gap between leadership theory and practice, you're not alone. And if you're ready to explore what it really takes to lead, not just in words but in actions, then this book is for you.

Welcome to "Authentic Leadership: What Really Works."

"Leadership is not about what you say; it's about what you do."

Table of Contents

Acknowledgements..

Foreword..

Chapter 1: The Leadership Myth...1

Chapter 2: Leadership Begins with You............................12

Chapter 3: The Power of Influence Over Authority........18

Chapter 4: Embracing Failure and Learning from It.....25

Chapter 5: The Importance of Grit and Persistence........32

Chapter 6: Authentic Communication................................38

Chapter 7: Leading Through Change................................45

Chapter 8: Building and Sustaining Trust........................51

Chapter 9: The Art of Delegation..57

Chapter 10: The Realities of Leading in a Corporate Environment..64

Chapter 11: The Role of Empathy in Leadership............72

Chapter 12: Sustaining Your Leadership Journey............80

Conclusion: Beyond the Buzzwords................................88

Leadership Self-Evaluation Worksheet............................93

Chapter 1:

The Leadership Myth

"The true measure of leadership is not found in titles or speeches, but in the actions taken when no one is watching."

Leadership. It's a word that's become almost meaningless through overuse. We see it emblazoned on book covers, touted in seminars, and plastered across motivational posters in break rooms. It's the topic of endless TED Talks and the subject of countless corporate initiatives. And yet, despite all the noise, how many of us can say we've truly experienced real leadership in our workplaces?

For most, the answer is disappointing.

The leadership industry is a multi-billion dollar machine, churning out advice, frameworks, and catchy slogans. But behind the glossy covers and the polished presentations, there's a harsh reality: many companies treat leadership as nothing more than a checkbox. It's something to talk about in meetings, to make everyone feel good about the direction we're heading, but it rarely translates into meaningful action.

The Cult of Leadership

The cult of leadership has grown so pervasive that it's easy to forget what leadership is really supposed to be. We've been conditioned to believe that leadership is about titles, authority, and charisma. We're told that if we follow the right steps, we can become the kind of leader who inspires others, drives change, and transforms organizations. But what's often missing from these promises is the truth that leadership isn't just about what you say—it's about what you do.

And that's where most leadership initiatives fall short.

The reality is that leadership isn't glamorous. It's not about standing on a stage and delivering a stirring speech. It's about making tough decisions, taking responsibility when things go wrong, and staying committed to your values even when it's inconvenient. It's about the small, everyday actions that build trust, inspire loyalty, and create real change.

Where Leadership Fails

Think back to the last leadership initiative you encountered. Maybe it was a new mission statement, a strategic vision, or a set of values rolled out by upper management. How did it play out? Did it change the way people worked? Did it inspire new levels of commitment and performance? Or did it fizzle out after the initial excitement wore off?

The problem with many leadership efforts is that they are often disconnected from the realities of the workplace. They're designed to look good on paper or to impress shareholders, but they fail to resonate with the people who are supposed to live them out every day. Leadership becomes more about appearances than actions.

A Personal Story

I've seen this play out in my own career. I remember one company I worked for that decided to launch a massive leadership development program. It was announced with much fanfare—complete with glossy brochures, inspirational videos, and a series of mandatory workshops. The message was clear: we were all going to become better leaders, and as a result, the company would achieve unprecedented success.

But as the months went by, it became clear that the program was all talk and no substance. The leadership principles we were taught in the workshops were never reflected in the decisions made by those at the top. The same old politics and power struggles continued, and the only thing that changed was the addition of a few more buzzwords to our corporate vocabulary.

The experience left me disillusioned, but it also taught me an important lesson: leadership isn't something you can package and sell. It's not a product, and it's not a one-size-fits-all solution. True leadership is messy, difficult, and often uncomfortable. It's about actions, not words, and it requires a level of honesty and authenticity that's often lacking in the corporate world.

The Leadership Myth

The myth of leadership is that it's something that can be easily taught, neatly packaged, and universally applied. But the truth is, leadership is deeply personal. What works for one person, in one context, may not work for another. And while it's important to learn from others, it's even more important to find your own way—to lead in a way that's true to who you are, rather than trying to conform to someone else's idea of what a leader should be.

In the chapters that follow, I'll share what I've learned about leading—not from books or seminars, but from the real-world challenges and experiences that have shaped my understanding of what it means to lead. It won't be a step-by-step guide, and it won't be filled with easy answers. Instead, it will be an honest exploration of the hard truths about leadership—truths that are often glossed over or ignored in the mainstream leadership discourse.

If you're looking for a quick fix or a magic formula, this book isn't for you. But if you're ready to challenge the myths of leadership and discover what it really takes to lead, then I invite you to keep reading. The journey won't be easy, but it will be worth it.

The Reality of Everyday Leadership

Leadership is often depicted as a grand, sweeping act—a charismatic CEO delivering an inspiring speech or a visionary entrepreneur launching a revolutionary product. But in reality, leadership is found in the mundane, in the small decisions made day after day, often without fanfare or recognition.

Real leadership happens in the quiet moments when no one is watching. It's when you choose to take the hard road because it's the right thing to do, even though the easier path would be more convenient. It's when you stay true to your values, even when it costs you something. It's about showing up, doing the work, and being consistent, especially when it's difficult.

Consider the role of a mid-level manager in a large corporation. They might not have the power to change company policy or the authority to dictate strategic direction. Yet, in their day-to-day interactions with their team, they have countless opportunities to lead—by listening to their employees, by providing support and guidance, and by setting an example of integrity and hard work. These actions may never make headlines, but they are the bedrock of effective leadership.

The Disconnect Between Theory and Practice

One of the biggest challenges in leadership is bridging the gap between theory and practice. Theories are often neat and tidy, presenting leadership as a series of steps or principles that can be easily applied in any situation. But real life is messy, unpredictable, and full of nuance that these theories often fail to capture.

For example, many leadership models emphasize the importance of empowering employees, fostering collaboration, and encouraging innovation. But what happens when you're leading a team through a crisis, when there's no time for consensus-building and tough decisions need to be made quickly? In these situations, the theoretical ideals of leadership can feel distant and impractical.

This doesn't mean that leadership theories are without value. They can provide useful frameworks and insights, and they often offer a starting point for developing your leadership style. But they must be adapted to fit the realities of the situation you're in. Leadership is not a one-size-fits-all endeavor, and what works in one context may not work in another.

The Weight of Responsibility

One of the hardest aspects of leadership is the weight of responsibility that comes with it. When you're a leader, your actions—or inactions—can have far-reaching consequences. People depend on you, and your decisions can impact their livelihoods, their careers, and their well-being.

This responsibility can be overwhelming at times, and it's not something that's often talked about in leadership seminars. We hear a lot about the rewards of leadership—the respect, the influence, the potential for making a difference—but less about the burdens that come with it.

True leadership requires the courage to face these burdens head-on. It means making difficult decisions, even when they're unpopular. It means taking responsibility when things go wrong, even if the failure wasn't entirely your fault. And it means being willing to make sacrifices for the good of your team or organization, even when it's personally challenging.

The Myth of the Perfect Leader

Another myth that pervades leadership culture is the idea of the "perfect leader"—someone who is always confident, always in control, and always knows the right thing to do. This ideal is not only unrealistic, but it's also damaging. It sets leaders up for failure, as they strive to meet impossible standards and feel inadequate when they inevitably fall short.

The truth is, no leader is perfect. We all have our weaknesses, our blind spots, and our moments of doubt. The most effective leaders are those who recognize their imperfections and learn to lead in spite of them. They don't pretend to have all the answers; instead, they seek out the wisdom and expertise of others. They are humble enough to admit when they're wrong and courageous enough to make tough calls, even when they're unsure of the outcome.

In the end, leadership is not about being perfect; it's about being real. It's about showing up authentically, with all your strengths and flaws, and leading with integrity. It's about being willing to do the hard work, to make the tough decisions, and to take responsibility for your actions.

Authenticity Over Image

In the corporate world, there's often a significant emphasis on projecting a certain image. Leaders are expected to appear confident, decisive, and in control at all times. This pressure to maintain a flawless image can lead to a disconnect between who leaders really are and the personas they feel they must present to the world.

But leadership is not about creating a perfect image. It's about being authentic, even when that authenticity reveals vulnerability or uncertainty. Authentic leaders are those who are willing to admit when they don't have all the answers, who are open about their challenges and struggles, and who lead not by projecting an idealized version of themselves, but by being real and relatable.

Authenticity builds trust. When people see that their leader is genuine, they are more likely to trust them and feel a deeper connection to them. This trust is crucial, especially in times of change or crisis, when employees need to know that they can rely on their leader to be honest and transparent.

However, being authentic in a corporate environment is not always easy. There are often pressures to conform to a certain leadership style or to downplay aspects of your personality that don't fit the corporate mold. But the most effective leaders are those who resist these pressures and stay true to who they are, even when it's difficult.

Staying True to Your Values

Leadership is often a test of values. It's easy to hold certain principles when everything is going smoothly, but the real challenge comes when those values are put to the test—when there's pressure to compromise for the sake of expediency, profit, or approval.

I've seen leaders who start their careers with strong values, only to see those values erode over time as they climb the corporate ladder. The demands of the job, the pressure to deliver results, and the desire to fit in with the company culture can all chip away at a leader's commitment to their principles.

But true leadership requires holding fast to your values, even when it's inconvenient or unpopular. It means making decisions that are aligned with your principles, even if those decisions are difficult or come with personal or professional costs. It's about leading with integrity, not just when it's easy, but especially when it's hard.

One of the most important lessons I've learned about leadership is that it's not about being liked or avoiding conflict; it's about doing what's right. This might mean standing up to a superior who is pushing for unethical behavior, or it might mean making a tough call that you know will be unpopular with your team. In these moments, your values will be your guide, helping you navigate the complexities of leadership with integrity.

The Price of Leadership

Leadership comes with a price. It's not just about the weight of responsibility or the challenges of staying true to your values; it's also about the personal sacrifices that often come with the role. These sacrifices might include long hours, the stress of difficult decisions, or the loneliness that can come from being at the top.

Many people aspire to leadership roles without fully understanding the toll it can take on their personal lives, their mental health, or their relationships. The pressure to perform, the scrutiny from others, and the constant demand to be "on" can be exhausting. And while leadership can be incredibly rewarding, it's important to recognize and prepare for the sacrifices that come with it.

But these sacrifices are also what make leadership meaningful. The challenges and hardships of leadership are what shape and refine you as a leader. They push you to grow, to become more resilient, and to develop a deeper understanding of yourself and others.

Conclusion: The Truth About Leadership

As we come to the end of this first chapter, it's clear that leadership is far from the glamorous ideal that is often presented in books and seminars. It's not about titles, image, or popularity. It's about authenticity, values, and the willingness to face difficult truths.

Leadership is messy, challenging, and often thankless. But it's also an opportunity to make a real difference—to influence others in a meaningful way, to stand up for what's right, and to leave a lasting impact on the people and organizations you lead.

In the chapters that follow, we'll explore these themes in greater depth, drawing from real-life experiences and practical insights. We'll look at what it really takes to lead, not just in theory, but in the day-to-day realities of work and life. And we'll challenge the myths and misconceptions that surround leadership, offering a more honest and realistic perspective on what it means to lead.

If you're ready to move beyond the leadership myths and explore the truth about what it takes to lead, then let's continue this journey together.

Chapter 2:

Leadership Begins with You

"Before you can lead others, you must first master the art of leading yourself."

When we think about leadership, our minds often jump to images of guiding others—of leading a team, a company, or a movement. But the foundation of all leadership isn't found in what you do for others; it's rooted in how you lead yourself. Before you can effectively lead others, you must first master the art of self-leadership.

The Pillar of Self-Awareness

Self-awareness is the cornerstone of self-leadership. It's the ability to understand your strengths, weaknesses, motivations, and the impact of your actions on others. Without self-awareness, it's easy to become blind to your own shortcomings, making it difficult to grow as a leader or to inspire trust in others.

Developing self-awareness requires a commitment to introspection. This might involve regular reflection, seeking feedback from others, or even engaging in mindfulness practices. The goal is to develop a clear and honest understanding of who you are, what drives you, and how you show up in different situations.

Self-awareness is not just about recognizing your strengths; it's also about acknowledging your weaknesses. Too often, leaders fall into the trap of focusing only on what they do well, while ignoring or downplaying their areas for improvement. But true self-leadership involves a willingness to confront your weaknesses head-on, to understand how they affect your leadership, and to take steps to address them.

The Importance of Personal Accountability

Leadership is often about making others accountable, but before you can hold others accountable, you must hold yourself accountable. Personal accountability means taking responsibility for your actions, decisions, and their outcomes. It means owning up to your mistakes, learning from them, and making the necessary changes to avoid repeating them.

One of the most common leadership pitfalls is the tendency to blame others when things go wrong. It's easy to point fingers at team members, external circumstances, or even company culture when a project fails or a goal isn't met. But effective leaders understand that, ultimately, the responsibility lies with them. They don't shy away from this responsibility; instead, they embrace it as an opportunity to learn and grow.

Personal accountability also extends to how you manage your time, energy, and priorities. As a leader, you set the tone for those around you. If you're consistently late, disorganized, or unfocused, it sends a message to your team that these behaviors are acceptable. On the other hand, when you hold yourself to high standards of accountability, you inspire others to do the same.

Leading by Example

One of the most powerful tools a leader has is their example. People are far more likely to follow what you do than what you say. If you want to cultivate certain behaviors, attitudes, or values in your team, you must first demonstrate them in your own actions.

This concept might seem straightforward, but in practice, it's often challenging. It requires consistency, discipline, and a commitment to living out the principles you espouse. For example, if you value transparency, you must be transparent in your communication, even when it's uncomfortable. If you value innovation, you must be willing to take risks and embrace change, even when it's uncertain.

Leading by example also means being willing to do the hard work. If you expect your team to go the extra mile, you must be prepared to do the same. This doesn't mean taking on every task yourself—delegation is an essential part of leadership—but it does mean showing that you're willing to roll up your sleeves and get involved when necessary.

The Role of Emotional Intelligence

Emotional intelligence (EI) is another critical aspect of self-leadership. EI is the ability to recognize, understand, and manage your own emotions, as well as the emotions of others. Leaders with high emotional intelligence are better equipped to navigate the complexities of human interactions, build strong relationships, and foster a positive work environment.

There are several components of emotional intelligence, including self-awareness (which we've already discussed), self-regulation, motivation, empathy, and social skills. Let's focus on a few of these in the context of self-leadership.

Self-Regulation: This involves managing your emotions, especially in stressful or challenging situations. Leaders who can regulate their emotions are able to remain calm, make rational decisions, and avoid acting impulsively. This ability to stay composed under pressure is crucial for maintaining the trust and confidence of your team.

Empathy: While empathy is often thought of in the context of leading others, it also plays a role in self-leadership. Empathy involves understanding the emotions and perspectives of others, which can help you navigate interpersonal dynamics more effectively. But it also means being kind and understanding toward yourself, especially when you face setbacks or challenges.

Motivation: Self-leadership requires a strong internal drive. Leaders who are motivated by a sense of purpose, rather than external rewards or recognition, are more resilient in the face of obstacles. This intrinsic motivation helps sustain the energy and commitment needed to lead effectively over the long term.

The Challenge of Consistency

Consistency is a key component of self-leadership. It's not enough to exhibit self-awareness, accountability, and emotional intelligence occasionally; these qualities must be consistently present in your leadership. Consistency builds trust and credibility, as it shows that you are reliable and dependable.

But consistency is also one of the most challenging aspects of self-leadership. Life is full of disruptions, stressors, and unexpected events that can throw you off balance. Maintaining consistency requires discipline and a commitment to your principles, even when it's difficult.

One way to cultivate consistency is by establishing routines and habits that reinforce your leadership qualities. This might involve setting aside time for reflection and self-assessment, regularly seeking feedback, or practicing mindfulness to stay grounded. By integrating these practices into your daily life, you create a strong foundation for consistent self-leadership.

Conclusion: The Foundation of Leadership

Self-leadership is the foundation upon which all other leadership is built. Without the ability to lead yourself, you cannot effectively lead others. It's about more than just setting a good example; it's about embodying the qualities and principles that you expect from those you lead.

In this chapter, we've explored the importance of self-awareness, personal accountability, emotional intelligence, and consistency. These qualities are not just important for leading others; they are essential for leading yourself. As you continue your leadership journey, remember that leadership begins with you. The more you invest in your own self-leadership, the more equipped you will be to lead others with authenticity, integrity, and impact.

Chapter 3:

The Power of Influence Over Authority

In the traditional view of leadership, authority is often seen as the ultimate source of power. Leaders are expected to wield their authority to direct, command, and control those beneath them. But true leadership doesn't come from the title on your business card or the position you hold in the hierarchy; it comes from your ability to influence others.

Understanding Influence vs. Authority

Authority is the formal power granted to a leader by their position. It's the ability to make decisions, allocate resources, and enforce rules. Authority is essential in any organization—it provides structure, ensures accountability, and enables leaders to make decisions that guide the organization toward its goals.

However, authority alone is limited. It can compel compliance, but it rarely inspires commitment. People might follow your orders because they have to, but that doesn't mean they believe in your vision or are motivated to give their best effort. This is where influence comes in.

Influence is the capacity to have an impact on the behaviors, attitudes, and opinions of others, not through coercion or control, but through persuasion, trust, and inspiration. While authority might get people to do what you want, influence makes them want to do it. The best leaders understand that influence is far more powerful and sustainable than authority.

"True leadership is earned through influence, not imposed through authority."

Building Trust: The Foundation of Influence

At the heart of influence is trust. Without trust, your ability to influence others is severely diminished. Trust is earned over time, through consistent actions, transparency, and a genuine concern for the well-being of those you lead.

Trust-building begins with honesty. Leaders who are open about their intentions, who communicate clearly and transparently, are more likely to earn the trust of their teams. This doesn't mean sharing every detail of every decision, but it does mean being truthful about your motives and acknowledging when you don't have all the answers.

Trust is also built through reliability. When you consistently follow through on your commitments, when your words match your actions, people learn that they can depend on you. This reliability fosters a sense of security, which in turn increases your influence.

Empathy plays a crucial role in building trust as well. When leaders demonstrate that they genuinely care about their team members—not just as employees, but as people—they create a connection that goes beyond the professional. This connection is a powerful source of influence, as people are more likely to follow leaders who they believe truly care about them.

Leading by Example: Influence in Action

One of the most effective ways to influence others is by leading by example. People are naturally drawn to leaders who embody the qualities and behaviors they aspire to. If you want your team to be diligent, committed, and ethical, you must first demonstrate these qualities yourself.

Leading by example is not just about working hard or being honest; it's about consistently aligning your actions with the values you espouse. This means making tough decisions that reflect your principles, even when it's easier to take shortcuts. It also means being willing to admit when you've made a mistake and taking responsibility for your actions.

When you lead by example, you create a culture of accountability and integrity within your team. Your actions set the standard for what is expected, and in doing so, you influence others to adopt those same standards. This form of influence is far more powerful than any directive you could issue.

The Role of Communication in Influence

Effective communication is another key to influence. Leaders who communicate well are able to convey their vision, articulate their expectations, and inspire their teams to achieve shared goals. But communication is not just about talking; it's also about listening.

Active listening is a crucial aspect of influential leadership. When you take the time to listen to others, you demonstrate respect for their ideas and perspectives. This not only builds trust but also allows you to understand the concerns, motivations, and aspirations of your team members. Armed with this understanding, you can tailor your approach to better influence and motivate them.

Communication also involves clarity. Leaders who communicate with clarity avoid confusion and ensure that everyone is on the same page. Clear communication reduces misunderstandings, aligns the team with the leader's vision, and provides a sense of direction. When people know what is expected of them and understand the rationale behind decisions, they are more likely to buy into the vision and commit to the work required to achieve it.

Inspiring Through Vision

One of the most powerful ways to influence others is by inspiring them with a compelling vision. A vision is more than just a goal or a target; it's a picture of the future that your team can rally around. A strong vision gives people a sense of purpose, something bigger than themselves that they can work toward.

To effectively inspire through vision, it's essential that the vision is both meaningful and achievable. It should resonate with the values and aspirations of your team, and it should be grounded in reality, with clear steps that can be taken to achieve it. Leaders who can articulate a vision that is both inspiring and practical are more likely to galvanize their teams and drive them toward success.

But inspiration isn't just about the end goal; it's also about the journey. Leaders who inspire influence their teams not just by painting a picture of the future, but by energizing them in the present. They bring passion and enthusiasm to their work, and they share that energy with others. This enthusiasm is contagious and can be a powerful motivator for those you lead.

The Long-Term Power of Influence

While authority can yield quick results, influence builds long-term commitment. When people are influenced rather than commanded, they are more likely to stay motivated, remain loyal, and go above and beyond in their work. Influence creates a deeper connection between the leader and the team, one that is built on mutual respect and shared values.

Influence also fosters innovation and creativity. When people feel empowered rather than controlled, they are more likely to take initiative, share their ideas, and contribute to the team's success. This kind of environment not only drives performance but also creates a culture where people are engaged and invested in their work.

Finally, influence is resilient. While authority can be undermined by changes in organizational structure or shifts in power, influence endures. It is based on relationships, trust, and mutual respect, which are not easily dismantled. This makes influence a far more sustainable form of leadership power.

Conclusion: Embracing the Power of Influence

As we conclude this chapter, it's clear that influence, not authority, is the true power of leadership. While authority has its place, it is influence that drives real, lasting change. By building trust, leading by example, communicating effectively, and inspiring through vision, leaders can cultivate influence that empowers their teams and creates a positive, dynamic work environment.

The chapters that follow will continue to explore the various facets of leadership, building on the foundation of self-leadership and influence we've established here. As you continue your leadership journey, remember that your ability to influence others will ultimately determine your effectiveness as a leader. Authority may get you compliance, but influence will win you commitment.

Chapter 4:

Embracing Failure and Learning from It

Failure. It's a word that most people dread, especially in the context of leadership. Leaders are often expected to succeed, to guide their teams to victory, and to make the right decisions. But the truth is, every leader will face failure at some point. The difference between effective and ineffective leaders lies not in whether they fail, but in how they respond to failure.

The Reality of Failure in Leadership

Failure is an inevitable part of leadership. Whether it's a project that didn't meet its goals, a strategy that fell flat, or a decision that backfired, every leader will experience setbacks. The key is to understand that failure is not a reflection of your worth as a leader; rather, it's an opportunity to learn, grow, and improve.

Too often, leaders fall into the trap of trying to avoid failure at all costs. They may play it safe, stick to the status quo, or refuse to take risks out of fear of failing. But this mindset not only stifles innovation and progress, it also limits personal and professional growth. In reality, some of the most valuable leadership lessons come from failure, not success.

Reframing Failure as a Learning Opportunity

One of the most important steps in embracing failure is to reframe it as a learning opportunity. Instead of viewing failure as a dead end, see it as a stepping stone on the path to success. When you approach failure with curiosity and a willingness to learn, you can extract valuable insights that will help you avoid similar mistakes in the future.

This shift in perspective requires humility and self-awareness. It's about acknowledging that you don't have all the answers and that mistakes are part of the journey. When you can openly admit to your failures and share the lessons you've learned, you set an example for others, creating a culture where learning and growth are prioritized over perfection.

Reframing failure also involves letting go of the fear of judgment. Many leaders worry that admitting to failure will undermine their authority or credibility. But in reality, being honest about your mistakes can enhance your credibility. It shows that you are human, that you are willing to take responsibility, and that you are committed to continuous improvement.

Analyzing Failure: The Post-Mortem Process

After experiencing a failure, it's important to take the time to analyze what went wrong and why. This is often referred to as a "post-mortem" process, where you dissect the failure to understand its root causes. The goal is not to assign blame, but to gain insights that can inform future decisions and actions.

During a post-mortem, ask yourself and your team questions such as:

- What were the original goals and expectations?

- What went well, and what didn't?

- Were there warning signs that were missed or ignored?

- What assumptions were made, and were they valid?

- What could have been done differently?

By answering these questions, you can identify patterns, uncover blind spots, and develop strategies for avoiding similar failures in the future. This process can also help you build resilience by normalizing failure as a part of the learning process.

It's important to approach the post-mortem with an open mind and a focus on improvement. Encourage your team to share their perspectives and insights, and be willing to listen without defensiveness. The more transparent and collaborative the process, the more valuable the lessons learned will be.

Building Resilience Through Failure

One of the most powerful outcomes of embracing failure is the development of resilience. Resilience is the ability to bounce back from setbacks, to adapt to challenges, and to keep moving forward in the face of adversity. It's a crucial quality for leaders, as it enables you to navigate the ups and downs of leadership without losing sight of your goals.

Resilience is not something you are born with; it's something you build over time, often through the experience of failure. Each time you face a setback and choose to learn from it rather than be defeated by it, you strengthen your resilience. Over time, you become more confident in your ability to handle challenges and more optimistic about your capacity to overcome obstacles.

Building resilience also involves cultivating a growth mindset. Leaders with a growth mindset believe that their abilities and intelligence can be developed through effort, learning, and persistence. They see challenges as opportunities to grow, rather than as threats to their competence. This mindset not only helps you recover from failure, but it also encourages you to take on new challenges and push the boundaries of what's possible.

Creating a Culture That Embraces Failure

As a leader, your attitude toward failure will set the tone for your team. If you view failure as something to be avoided at all costs, your team will likely adopt the same mindset. This can lead to a culture of risk aversion, where people are afraid to take chances or innovate for fear of making mistakes.

On the other hand, if you embrace failure as a natural part of the learning process, you create an environment where experimentation, creativity, and innovation are encouraged. In such a culture, team members feel safe to take risks, share new ideas, and challenge the status quo, knowing that failure will be met with support and a focus on learning rather than punishment.

Creating a culture that embraces failure starts with leading by example. Be open about your own failures and the lessons you've learned from them. Encourage your team to share their own experiences with failure, and celebrate the learning that comes from taking risks, even when those risks don't pay off.

It's also important to provide support and resources for your team to learn from their failures. This might involve offering training, mentorship, or opportunities for professional development. By investing in your team's growth, you reinforce the idea that failure is not an endpoint, but a step toward greater success.

The Long-Term Benefits of Embracing Failure

Embracing failure has long-term benefits for both you and your organization. Leaders who learn from their failures become more skilled, more adaptable, and more effective over time. They develop a deeper understanding of themselves and their work, and they are better equipped to navigate the complexities of leadership.

For organizations, a culture that embraces failure fosters innovation, agility, and continuous improvement. It enables the organization to stay competitive in a rapidly changing world, as team members are empowered to explore new ideas and take calculated risks. In the long run, this leads to greater resilience, creativity, and success.

Conclusion: Embracing Failure as a Path to Growth

As we conclude this chapter, it's clear that failure is not something to be feared, but something to be embraced. It's an essential part of the leadership journey, offering opportunities for learning, growth, and the development of resilience. By reframing failure as a learning opportunity, analyzing it with an open mind, and creating a culture that supports risk-taking, you can turn setbacks into stepping stones on the path to success.

In the chapters that follow, we will continue to explore the challenges and opportunities of leadership, building on the lessons learned from failure. Remember, every failure is a chance to grow, to improve, and to become a more effective leader. Embrace it, learn from it, and use it to propel yourself and your team forward.

"Failure is not the end; it's the beginning of your greatest growth."

Chapter 5:

The Importance of Grit and Persistence

"Success is not about how fast you reach the top, but how steadfastly you climb when the path gets steep."

In leadership, as in life, success is rarely achieved overnight. It's often the result of sustained effort, overcoming obstacles, and pushing through challenges that would cause others to give up. This ability to persevere in the face of adversity is what we call grit, and it is one of the most crucial qualities a leader can possess.

Defining Grit

Grit is the combination of passion and perseverance toward long-term goals. It's the determination to keep going, even when the path is difficult, and the unwavering commitment to see something through to the end. Unlike talent or intelligence, which are often viewed as innate qualities, grit is something that can be cultivated and developed over time.

In leadership, grit manifests in the ability to stay focused on your vision, to keep pushing forward despite setbacks, and to maintain your enthusiasm and drive even when progress is slow. Leaders with grit are not easily discouraged by failure or frustration; they understand that the road to success is often paved with challenges, and they are willing to do the hard work necessary to achieve their goals.

The Role of Persistence in Leadership

Persistence is the active expression of grit. It's the day-to-day effort that leaders put into achieving their objectives, even when the initial excitement has worn off and the work becomes tedious or difficult. Persistence is what keeps leaders moving forward when others might be tempted to give up.

One of the key aspects of persistence is the ability to stay committed to your goals over the long term. This doesn't mean blindly sticking to a plan that isn't working, but rather being adaptable and resilient in the face of challenges. Persistent leaders are able to adjust their strategies as needed, but they never lose sight of their ultimate goals.

Persistence also involves a willingness to put in the necessary time and effort to see a project or initiative through to completion. This can be especially challenging in a world that often values quick results and instant gratification. But true leadership requires a long-term perspective, and persistent leaders understand that real success takes time and sustained effort.

The Grit to Push Through Challenges

Every leader will face challenges that test their resolve. Whether it's a difficult project, a crisis within the organization, or resistance from others, these challenges can be daunting. But it's in these moments that grit becomes most valuable.

Grit enables leaders to push through challenges by keeping their focus on the bigger picture. It's the ability to see beyond the immediate obstacles and maintain a strong sense of purpose. Leaders with grit are not easily deterred by setbacks; instead, they view challenges as opportunities to grow and improve.

One of the most important aspects of grit is the ability to stay motivated, even when progress is slow. It's easy to feel enthusiastic when things are going well, but true grit is demonstrated when you can maintain that same level of motivation during tough times. This requires a deep commitment to your goals and a belief in the value of your work.

Cultivating Grit and Persistence

Grit and persistence are not qualities that people are born with; they are developed through experience and practice. As a leader, you can cultivate these qualities by embracing challenges, setting long-term goals, and committing to the process of continuous improvement.

One way to develop grit is by setting goals that are both challenging and meaningful. When your goals align with your values and passions, you are more likely to stay committed to them, even when the going gets tough. It's also important to break down your long-term goals into smaller, manageable steps, which can help you maintain momentum and see progress along the way.

Another important aspect of cultivating grit is learning to manage setbacks effectively. Instead of viewing failures as reasons to give up, persistent leaders see them as opportunities to learn and grow. They analyze what went wrong, adjust their approach, and keep moving forward.

Building a support network can also be instrumental in developing persistence. Surround yourself with people who encourage and challenge you, who can offer perspective when you're feeling discouraged, and who share your commitment to long-term success. This network can provide the motivation and accountability you need to keep going when things get tough.

The Long-Term Impact of Grit in Leadership

Grit has a profound impact on both the leader and the organization. Leaders who demonstrate grit and persistence inspire those around them to do the same. Their ability to stay focused and motivated in the face of challenges creates a culture of resilience and determination within their teams.

Over time, the impact of grit can be seen in the leader's achievements. Persistent leaders are often the ones who bring their visions to life, who turn ideas into reality, and who drive their organizations to success. They are not deterred by obstacles or delays; instead, they are motivated by them, using each challenge as an opportunity to strengthen their resolve and refine their strategies.

The long-term impact of grit is also evident in the personal growth of the leader. Each challenge overcome, each setback turned into a learning opportunity, contributes to the development of stronger leadership skills. Leaders with grit are more confident, more resilient, and more capable of navigating the complexities of leadership.

Conclusion: The Enduring Power of Grit and Persistence

As we conclude this chapter, it's clear that grit and persistence are essential qualities for effective leadership. While talent, intelligence, and strategy are important, it is grit—the combination of passion and perseverance—that ultimately determines a leader's success.

In the chapters that follow, we will continue to explore the qualities and skills that are necessary for effective leadership. Remember that grit is not about being perfect or never facing challenges; it's about having the determination to keep going, to learn from your experiences, and to stay committed to your goals, no matter what obstacles you encounter.

Leadership is a journey, and grit is the fuel that keeps you moving forward. Cultivate it, nurture it, and let it guide you as you lead your team toward success.

Chapter 6:

Authentic Communication

Communication is the lifeblood of leadership. It's how leaders share their vision, set expectations, and connect with their teams. But not all communication is created equal. The most effective leaders don't just communicate frequently; they communicate authentically. Authentic communication is about being clear, honest, and empathetic—qualities that build trust, foster collaboration, and drive successful outcomes.

The Core of Authentic Communication: Honesty

At the heart of authentic communication is honesty. Leaders who communicate honestly earn the trust of their teams, because people know that what they say can be relied upon. Honesty in communication means being truthful about the realities of the situation, even when the truth is uncomfortable or difficult to hear.

Honesty also involves transparency. Transparent leaders share information openly, keeping their teams informed about what's happening, why decisions are being made, and what the future may hold. This openness helps to create a culture of trust and accountability, where people feel respected and valued because they are kept in the loop.

However, honesty doesn't mean being blunt or insensitive. It's about finding the right balance between being truthful and being considerate of how your words will impact others. The best leaders are those who can deliver difficult messages with both honesty and compassion, ensuring that their communication is clear, but also mindful of the emotions and perspectives of those on the receiving end.

The Importance of Clarity

Clarity is another essential component of authentic communication. When leaders communicate with clarity, they minimize misunderstandings, ensure that everyone is on the same page, and provide a clear direction for their teams to follow. Clarity in communication involves being precise, concise, and consistent in the messages you deliver.

One of the biggest barriers to clarity in communication is jargon. While technical language and industry-specific terms may be necessary in some contexts, overusing jargon can create confusion and alienate those who are not familiar with the terminology. Authentic communicators strive to use language that is accessible and easy to understand, ensuring that their messages are clear to everyone involved.

Clarity also extends to setting expectations. When leaders are clear about what they expect from their teams—whether it's in terms of performance, behavior, or goals—they provide a roadmap that guides their team's actions. This not only helps to align efforts but also reduces the likelihood of mistakes or miscommunication down the line.

"Authentic communication is the bridge between trust and action."

The Role of Empathy in Communication

Empathy is the ability to understand and share the feelings of others, and it plays a crucial role in authentic communication. When leaders communicate with empathy, they demonstrate that they care about the people they are leading. This fosters a sense of connection and trust, which are essential for effective leadership.

Empathetic communication involves actively listening to others, seeking to understand their perspectives, and responding in a way that acknowledges their feelings and concerns. It's about putting yourself in someone else's shoes and considering how your words will impact them.

Empathy also requires patience. In conversations where emotions are high or where there is disagreement, it's important to take the time to listen carefully, to ask questions, and to avoid jumping to conclusions. By showing that you are genuinely interested in understanding the other person's point of view, you create an environment where open, honest, and productive communication can occur.

Listening: The Other Side of Communication

Effective communication is not just about talking; it's also about listening. In fact, listening is one of the most important aspects of authentic communication, yet it is often overlooked. Leaders who are good listeners are better able to understand the needs, concerns, and motivations of their teams, which enables them to respond more effectively.

Active listening involves more than just hearing the words being spoken; it requires paying attention to the speaker's tone, body language, and underlying emotions. It's about being fully present in the conversation, without distractions, and showing that you value what the other person has to say.

One way to practice active listening is by reflecting back what you've heard. This can be as simple as summarizing the speaker's points or asking clarifying questions to ensure that you've understood correctly. Reflecting back not only demonstrates that you're engaged in the conversation, but it also helps to prevent misunderstandings and shows that you respect the other person's input.

The Impact of Authentic Communication on Team Dynamics

Authentic communication has a profound impact on team dynamics. When leaders communicate honestly, clearly, and empathetically, they create an environment of trust and openness. This encourages team members to share their ideas, voice their concerns, and collaborate more effectively.

In a team where authentic communication is the norm, people feel safe to express themselves without fear of judgment or retaliation. This psychological safety is critical for fostering innovation, creativity, and problem-solving. It also helps to build strong relationships within the team, as people feel respected and valued for their contributions.

Moreover, authentic communication helps to prevent and resolve conflicts. When team members know that they can approach their leader with issues and that those issues will be addressed fairly and transparently, conflicts are less likely to escalate. And when conflicts do arise, authentic communication provides a foundation for finding solutions that are acceptable to all parties involved.

The Challenges of Authentic Communication

While authentic communication is incredibly powerful, it's not always easy. Leaders may face various challenges, such as the fear of delivering bad news, the pressure to maintain a certain image, or the temptation to withhold information to avoid conflict. However, these challenges can be overcome with practice and a commitment to honesty, clarity, and empathy.

One common challenge is the need to balance honesty with tact. Leaders must be truthful, but they must also be considerate of how their messages will be received. This requires emotional intelligence and a deep understanding of the people you are communicating with.

Another challenge is managing communication in times of uncertainty. When leaders don't have all the answers, it can be tempting to avoid communicating altogether. However, silence can breed anxiety and mistrust. In such situations, it's better to communicate openly about what is known, what is unknown, and what steps are being taken to address the uncertainty. This approach fosters transparency and helps to maintain trust, even in difficult times.

Conclusion: The Power of Authentic Communication

As we conclude this chapter, it's clear that authentic communication is a cornerstone of effective leadership. By communicating with honesty, clarity, empathy, and active listening, leaders can build trust, foster collaboration, and create a positive and productive team environment.

In the chapters that follow, we will continue to explore the qualities and practices that make for successful leadership. Remember that authentic communication is not just about what you say, but also about how you listen and connect with others. It's a powerful tool for building relationships, resolving conflicts, and leading with integrity.

Leadership is about more than just giving orders or making decisions; it's about connecting with people, understanding their needs, and guiding them toward a common goal. Authentic communication is the key to making those connections and leading with impact.

Chapter 7:

Leading Through Change

Change is a constant in both life and leadership. Whether it's a shift in organizational strategy, the introduction of new technology, or a significant market disruption, leaders are often called upon to guide their teams through transitions. Leading through change is one of the most challenging aspects of leadership, but it's also one of the most important. How leaders handle change can determine the success or failure of an organization.

The Nature of Change

Change can take many forms. It might be planned, such as a strategic shift within the organization, or it might be unexpected, like a sudden economic downturn or a global pandemic. Regardless of its nature, change often brings uncertainty, discomfort, and resistance. People naturally resist change because it disrupts the status quo and introduces the unknown.

For leaders, the challenge is to manage this resistance and help their teams navigate the uncertainty that comes with change. This requires not only strategic thinking but also emotional intelligence, empathy, and strong communication skills.

The Leader's Role in Change Management

As a leader, your role in managing change is multifaceted. You need to be a strategist, a communicator, a motivator, and a supporter. Your team will look to you for guidance, stability, and reassurance, especially when the future seems uncertain.

One of the first steps in leading through change is to establish a clear vision of what the change will achieve and why it's necessary. This vision serves as a beacon that guides the organization through the transition. It helps people understand the purpose behind the change and what the desired outcome is. When people see the value and the potential benefits of the change, they are more likely to get on board.

However, simply having a vision is not enough. You need to communicate it effectively and repeatedly. Change can be overwhelming, and people may not fully grasp the implications the first time they hear about it. It's your job to ensure that the vision is understood and that it resonates with your team. This requires clear, consistent, and empathetic communication.

Managing Resistance to Change

Resistance to change is natural and should be expected. People may fear losing their jobs, their status, or their routines. They may worry about their ability to adapt to new systems or processes. As a leader, it's important to acknowledge these fears and address them head-on.

One effective way to manage resistance is to involve people in the change process. When team members feel that they have a voice in the transition, they are more likely to support it. This might involve soliciting feedback, involving key stakeholders in planning, or allowing team members to contribute ideas for how the change can be implemented.

It's also important to be transparent about the challenges and risks associated with the change. Trying to downplay or ignore potential difficulties can lead to mistrust and increased resistance. Instead, be honest about what's at stake and what the organization will need to overcome. This transparency helps to build trust and credibility, even in the face of difficult changes.

The Importance of Adaptability

Adaptability is a crucial quality for leaders during times of change. Change often requires leaders to step out of their comfort zones, to think creatively, and to be willing to adjust their strategies as new information becomes available. The ability to pivot and adapt quickly is what separates effective leaders from those who struggle in times of transition.

Adaptability also involves being open to new ideas and approaches. Change often brings opportunities for innovation, and leaders who are willing to embrace these opportunities can help their organizations thrive in the new environment. This might involve experimenting with new processes, exploring new markets, or adopting new technologies.

However, adaptability doesn't mean abandoning your principles or vision at the first sign of trouble. It's about finding the right balance between staying true to your core values and being flexible enough to adjust your approach as needed. This balance is key to navigating change successfully.

Supporting Your Team Through Change

Leading through change is not just about managing processes; it's also about supporting people. Change can be stressful, and it's important to recognize the emotional impact it can have on your team. As a leader, you need to provide both practical support and emotional support.

Practical support might involve providing the necessary training and resources to help your team adapt to new systems or processes. It might also involve adjusting workloads or timelines to give people the space they need to get comfortable with the changes.

Emotional support involves being there for your team, listening to their concerns, and offering reassurance. It's important to show empathy and understanding, acknowledging that change can be difficult and that it's okay to feel uncertain or anxious. By creating a supportive environment, you help your team build the resilience they need to navigate the transition.

One way to provide support is by celebrating small wins along the way. Change can be a long and challenging process, and recognizing progress—no matter how small—can boost morale and keep your team motivated.

The Long-Term Benefits of Embracing Change

While change can be challenging, it also brings opportunities for growth, innovation, and improvement. Leaders who embrace change and guide their teams through it effectively can position their organizations for long-term success. Change forces organizations to adapt, to rethink their strategies, and to find new ways to create value.

For leaders, successfully navigating change can also lead to personal and professional growth. It challenges you to develop new skills, to think creatively, and to strengthen your leadership abilities. The experience of leading through change can make you a more resilient, adaptable, and effective leader.

Conclusion: Leading with Resilience and Vision

As we conclude this chapter, it's clear that leading through change is one of the most demanding yet rewarding aspects of leadership. It requires a clear vision, strong communication, adaptability, and a deep understanding of the people you lead. By embracing change and guiding your team with resilience and empathy, you can turn challenges into opportunities and drive your organization toward a successful future.

In the chapters that follow, we will continue to explore the qualities and practices that are essential for effective leadership. Remember that change is inevitable, but how you lead through it will define your success as a leader.

Leadership is not just about maintaining the status quo; it's about navigating the unknown, embracing new possibilities, and leading your team with confidence and vision through whatever changes come your way.

"Change is inevitable; how you lead through it defines your legacy."

Chapter 8:

Building and Sustaining Trust

"Trust is the foundation upon which all successful leadership is built."

Trust is the foundation of effective leadership. Without trust, no team can function effectively, and no leader can truly inspire or motivate others. Building and sustaining trust is not a one-time effort but a continuous process that requires integrity, transparency, and consistent actions. This chapter delves into how trust is established, maintained, and, when necessary, rebuilt.

The Importance of Trust in Leadership

Trust is the glue that holds teams together. It's what enables people to work collaboratively, take risks, and support one another. When trust is present, team members feel safe to express their ideas, share concerns, and engage fully in their work. Conversely, when trust is lacking, communication breaks down, collaboration falters, and the team's effectiveness is compromised.

For leaders, trust is essential for gaining the commitment and loyalty of their team members. People are more likely to follow and support a leader they trust, even in difficult times. Trust also empowers leaders to delegate responsibilities confidently, knowing that their team will act in the organization's best interest.

Building Trust: The Foundation

Building trust begins with integrity. Leaders who act with integrity are honest, ethical, and consistent in their actions. They do what they say they will do, and they uphold their values, even when it's challenging. Integrity creates a strong foundation for trust because it shows that you are reliable and that your words and actions align.

Another key element of building trust is transparency. Leaders who are transparent share information openly and honestly. They communicate not just the good news, but also the challenges and uncertainties. This openness helps to build credibility and shows that you respect your team enough to keep them informed.

Consistency is also crucial for building trust. When leaders are consistent in their actions and decisions, it creates a sense of predictability and stability. Team members know what to expect and can rely on their leader to act in a manner that aligns with the organization's values and goals.

The Role of Vulnerability in Trust

Vulnerability is often seen as a weakness, but in leadership, it can be a powerful tool for building trust. When leaders are willing to show vulnerability—whether by admitting a mistake, asking for help, or acknowledging uncertainty—they demonstrate authenticity and humility. This openness encourages team members to do the same, creating an environment where trust can flourish.

Vulnerability also fosters deeper connections between leaders and their teams. It shows that you are human, that you don't have all the answers, and that you value the contributions of others. This creates a culture of mutual respect and trust, where people feel comfortable being themselves and taking risks.

Maintaining Trust: Consistency and Accountability

Building trust is only the first step; maintaining it requires ongoing effort. One of the most important aspects of maintaining trust is consistency. Leaders must consistently act in ways that align with their values and the expectations they have set. Inconsistency—whether in decision-making, communication, or behavior—can quickly erode trust.

Accountability is another key factor in sustaining trust. Leaders who hold themselves accountable for their actions, who admit when they are wrong, and who take responsibility for their mistakes, strengthen the trust their team has in them. This accountability extends to following through on commitments and being reliable in all aspects of leadership.

Communication plays a vital role in maintaining trust as well. Regular, open communication keeps the lines of trust strong. It ensures that team members are informed, that their concerns are heard, and that they feel valued. Leaders who make communication a priority demonstrate that they are invested in maintaining the trust of their team.

Rebuilding Trust: The Path to Recovery

Even the most trusted leaders can make mistakes, and when trust is broken, it can be challenging to rebuild. However, rebuilding trust is possible with time, effort, and the right approach.

The first step in rebuilding trust is to acknowledge the breach. Whether it's a broken promise, a miscommunication, or a decision that didn't align with the team's values, it's important to own up to the mistake. Apologize sincerely, and take responsibility for the impact your actions have had.

Next, take corrective action. Show through your actions that you are committed to making things right. This might involve making amends, changing your behavior, or putting new processes in place to prevent similar issues in the future. Consistent, positive actions over time are key to rebuilding trust.

Transparency is also critical in the process of rebuilding trust. Be open about what went wrong, why it happened, and what you are doing to address it. Keep the lines of communication open, and invite feedback from your team. This openness can help to rebuild credibility and show that you are committed to restoring trust.

Finally, be patient. Rebuilding trust takes time, and it cannot be rushed. It requires a sustained effort to demonstrate that the breach was an exception, not the norm, and that you are dedicated to re-establishing a trusting relationship.

The Long-Term Impact of Trust in Leadership

Trust is not just a nice-to-have in leadership; it's a critical component of long-term success. Leaders who build and maintain trust create teams that are more cohesive, more collaborative, and more effective. Trust enables teams to work together more smoothly, to innovate more freely, and to achieve their goals more efficiently.

For leaders, the impact of trust is seen in the loyalty and commitment of their team members. Trustworthy leaders inspire others to go above and beyond, to stay with the organization through challenging times, and to invest their best efforts in their work. This loyalty and dedication are invaluable assets for any organization.

In the long term, trust also enhances a leader's reputation. Leaders who are known for their integrity, transparency, and reliability are more likely to be respected and admired, both within their organization and in the broader industry. This reputation can open doors to new opportunities and strengthen the leader's influence and effectiveness.

Conclusion: The Pillar of Trust

As we conclude this chapter, it's clear that trust is the pillar upon which effective leadership is built. Without trust, no leader can truly inspire, motivate, or lead their team to success. By focusing on building, maintaining, and, when necessary, rebuilding trust, leaders can create a strong foundation for their leadership and for their organization's success.

In the chapters that follow, we will continue to explore the qualities and practices that are essential for effective leadership. Remember that trust is not something that can be taken for granted; it must be earned, nurtured, and protected. As a leader, your ability to build and sustain trust will define your success and the success of your team.

Leadership is about more than just making decisions or giving orders; it's about building relationships, earning trust, and leading with integrity. Trust is the currency of leadership, and it's what allows you to inspire and guide others toward a common goal.

Chapter 9:

The Art of Delegation

Delegation is one of the most powerful tools in a leader's arsenal, yet it's often one of the most underutilized. Effective delegation allows leaders to focus on their most important tasks, empowers team members to take ownership of their work, and drives overall organizational success. However, delegation is not just about handing off tasks; it's about entrusting responsibilities in a way that maximizes both individual and team potential.

Why Delegation Matters

At its core, delegation is about trust. When leaders delegate, they are expressing confidence in their team members' abilities to take on important tasks and make meaningful contributions. This trust not only empowers individuals but also fosters a sense of ownership and accountability within the team.

Delegation also allows leaders to focus on the bigger picture. By delegating tasks that others are capable of handling, leaders free up their time to concentrate on strategic thinking, decision-making, and other high-priority activities that require their attention. This shift in focus is essential for effective leadership, as it ensures that leaders are not bogged down by details that can be managed by others.

Moreover, delegation is a powerful tool for developing the skills and capabilities of team members. When given the opportunity to take on new responsibilities, individuals can grow, learn, and expand their expertise. This not only benefits the individual but also strengthens the overall team by building a more skilled and versatile workforce.

The Challenges of Delegation

Despite its many benefits, delegation can be challenging for some leaders. One common challenge is the fear of losing control. Leaders who are used to being deeply involved in every aspect of their work may find it difficult to let go and trust others to handle important tasks. This can lead to micromanagement, which undermines the benefits of delegation and can erode trust within the team.

Another challenge is the misconception that delegation is simply about offloading tasks. Effective delegation requires careful consideration of who is best suited for the task, clear communication of expectations, and ongoing support to ensure success. Without these elements, delegation can result in misunderstandings, mistakes, and missed opportunities.

Finally, some leaders may struggle with delegation because they feel that it's faster or easier to do the work themselves. While this may be true in the short term, it's a shortsighted approach that can lead to burnout and hinder the growth of the team. True leadership involves investing in the development of others, even if it requires more time and effort upfront.

How to Delegate Effectively

Effective delegation begins with understanding what to delegate. Not every task is suitable for delegation, and leaders must carefully consider which responsibilities can be entrusted to others. Tasks that are routine, time-consuming, or fall within someone else's area of expertise are often good candidates for delegation. Conversely, tasks that require the leader's unique skills, experience, or authority should typically remain under their direct control.

Once you've identified tasks that can be delegated, the next step is to choose the right person for the job.

Consider the skills, experience, and workload of your team members, and select someone who is well-suited to handle the responsibility. Delegation is also an opportunity to stretch your team members' capabilities, so don't be afraid to assign tasks that will challenge them and help them grow.

Clear communication is essential for effective delegation. When delegating a task, provide all the necessary information, including the objectives, deadlines, and any specific requirements. Make sure the person understands what is expected of them and how their work fits into the larger goals of the team or organization. It's also important to communicate the level of authority they have in making decisions related to the task.

Delegation doesn't end with the assignment of a task. Providing support and guidance throughout the process is crucial to ensuring success. Be available to answer questions, provide feedback, and offer assistance as needed. However, it's also important to avoid micromanaging. Trust your team member to do the work, and resist the temptation to take over if things aren't going exactly as you envisioned.

"Delegation is not about giving away tasks; it's about empowering others to grow."

Empowering Through Delegation

Delegation is not just about getting work done; it's about empowering your team. When you delegate effectively, you give your team members the opportunity to take ownership of their work, to make decisions, and to contribute in meaningful ways. This empowerment can lead to increased motivation, job satisfaction, and a greater sense of responsibility.

Empowering your team through delegation also fosters a culture of collaboration and innovation. When people feel trusted and valued, they are more likely to share ideas, take initiative, and seek out new ways to contribute. This dynamic not only benefits the individual but also drives the overall success of the organization.

Delegation also plays a critical role in succession planning. By giving team members the opportunity to develop new skills and take on leadership roles, you are preparing them for future advancement within the organization. This helps to ensure continuity and stability, as you are building a pipeline of capable leaders who can step up when needed.

Overcoming Delegation Pitfalls

While delegation is a powerful tool, it's important to be aware of potential pitfalls and how to overcome them. One common pitfall is over-delegation, where too much responsibility is offloaded onto team members without adequate support or resources. This can lead to burnout, frustration, and decreased morale. To avoid this, be mindful of your team's capacity and ensure that you are providing the necessary support to help them succeed.

Another pitfall is under-delegation, where leaders hold onto too many tasks and fail to delegate effectively. This can result in missed opportunities for growth, both for the leader and the team. To overcome this, regularly assess your workload and look for tasks that can be delegated. Remember that delegation is not a sign of weakness; it's a strategic decision that enables you to focus on what matters most.

Finally, be aware of the "delegate and forget" trap, where tasks are delegated but not followed up on. Effective delegation requires ongoing communication and feedback. Check in with your team members regularly to see how they are progressing, offer guidance, and provide recognition for their efforts.

The Long-Term Benefits of Delegation

Effective delegation has long-term benefits for both the leader and the organization. For leaders, delegation frees up time to focus on strategic priorities, reduces stress, and prevents burnout. It also helps to build a stronger, more capable team, as individuals are given the opportunity to develop new skills and take on greater responsibilities.

For the organization, delegation fosters a culture of trust, collaboration, and innovation. It encourages people to take initiative, to share their ideas, and to contribute to the organization's success in meaningful ways. This dynamic environment is essential for achieving long-term goals and maintaining a competitive edge.

Conclusion: The Art of Delegation

As we conclude this chapter, it's clear that delegation is not just a task management strategy; it's an art that requires careful thought, clear communication, and a commitment to empowering others. When done effectively, delegation can drive individual growth, team success, and organizational excellence.

In the chapters that follow, we will continue to explore the qualities and practices that are essential for effective leadership. Remember that delegation is a powerful tool that can help you achieve more by leveraging the strengths and talents of your team. By mastering the art of delegation, you can lead with greater impact, focus on what matters most, and create a dynamic, empowered team that is poised for success.

Leadership is about more than just doing the work yourself; it's about guiding, supporting, and empowering others to achieve their full potential. Delegation is key to making that happen.

Chapter 10:

The Realities of Leading in a Corporate Environment

"Navigating the corporate maze requires both strategy and integrity."

Leading in a corporate environment presents a unique set of challenges. Unlike smaller organizations or entrepreneurial ventures, corporations often come with layers of bureaucracy, complex hierarchies, and internal politics that can complicate decision-making and leadership. In this chapter, we'll explore the realities of leading in such an environment and how to navigate these challenges while staying true to your leadership principles.

Understanding Corporate Bureaucracy

Bureaucracy is a common feature of large organizations. It provides structure and consistency, ensuring that processes are followed, and decisions are made according to established protocols. However, bureaucracy can also be a double-edged sword. While it can bring order, it can also create inefficiencies, slow down decision-making, and stifle innovation.

As a leader in a corporate environment, it's important to understand the role of bureaucracy and how to work within it effectively. This means recognizing when to follow established processes and when to challenge them. It also involves finding ways to streamline procedures and cut through red tape to keep your team agile and responsive.

One of the keys to navigating bureaucracy is building relationships with key stakeholders who have influence within the organization. By cultivating these relationships, you can gain support for your initiatives and find allies who can help you navigate the complexities of the corporate structure.

Navigating Corporate Politics

Corporate politics are an inevitable part of life in a large organization. Politics often revolve around power, influence, and competing interests, and they can significantly impact your ability to lead effectively. Understanding and navigating these politics is essential for achieving your goals and maintaining your integrity as a leader.

To navigate corporate politics successfully, it's important to be aware of the informal networks and power dynamics at play within your organization. This involves understanding who holds influence, how decisions are made, and what the underlying motivations of key players are. By being politically savvy, you can position yourself and your team in a way that aligns with the broader organizational goals while avoiding unnecessary conflicts.

However, navigating politics doesn't mean compromising your values or engaging in unethical behavior. It's about being strategic in your approach, building alliances, and understanding the landscape so you can effectively advocate for your team and your initiatives.

Balancing Short-Term Pressures with Long-Term Vision

One of the biggest challenges in a corporate environment is balancing the short-term pressures of meeting quarterly targets with the long-term vision for your team or organization. Corporations are often driven by the need to deliver immediate results, which can lead to a focus on short-term gains at the expense of long-term sustainability.

As a leader, it's your responsibility to manage these pressures while staying true to your vision. This might involve making difficult decisions, such as prioritizing long-term investments over short-term profitability or advocating for initiatives that may not show immediate returns but are critical for future success.

Balancing short-term and long-term goals requires clear communication with your team and your superiors. It's important to articulate the rationale behind your decisions and to build a case for why a long-term approach will ultimately benefit the organization. By aligning your vision with the broader goals of the company, you can create a compelling narrative that supports both short-term success and long-term growth.

Staying True to Your Principles

Corporate environments can sometimes challenge a leader's principles. Whether it's pressure to compromise on ethical standards, to conform to the status quo, or to prioritize profits over people, leaders in corporations often face difficult choices that test their integrity.

Staying true to your principles in a corporate environment requires a strong sense of self-awareness and a commitment to your core values. It's about knowing what you stand for and being willing to stand up for those principles, even when it's difficult.

One of the most effective ways to stay true to your principles is to lead by example. By consistently demonstrating your values through your actions, you set a standard for your team and show that it's possible to succeed in a corporate environment without compromising your integrity. This can also help to build a culture of trust and respect within your team, as people see that you are a leader who practices what you preach.

When faced with situations that challenge your principles, it's important to seek guidance and support from trusted mentors or colleagues. Sometimes, having a sounding board can help you navigate complex situations and reinforce your commitment to doing the right thing.

Managing Change in a Corporate Environment

Change is a constant in the corporate world, whether it's a shift in market conditions, a merger or acquisition, or a new strategic direction. Leading through change in a corporate environment requires a combination of adaptability, resilience, and clear communication.

One of the key challenges of managing change in a corporate setting is dealing with the resistance that often accompanies it. People may resist change because they fear the unknown, are comfortable with the status quo, or are skeptical of the benefits. As a leader, it's your role to address these concerns, communicate the reasons for the change, and help your team navigate the transition.

Clear communication is critical during times of change. It's important to provide as much information as possible, to be transparent about what is happening and why, and to keep the lines of communication open. This helps to build trust and reduces the uncertainty that can cause anxiety and resistance.

It's also important to be resilient in the face of setbacks. Change is rarely a smooth process, and there will likely be bumps along the way. By staying focused on the end goal, being flexible in your approach, and supporting your team through the transition, you can help to ensure that the change is successful.

Leveraging Corporate Resources

One of the advantages of leading in a corporate environment is access to a wide range of resources, including financial capital, technology, and expertise. Effective leaders know how to leverage these resources to drive their initiatives and achieve their goals.

To make the most of corporate resources, it's important to build strong relationships with other departments and functions within the organization. By collaborating with finance, IT, HR, and other teams, you can access the support and expertise you need to execute your strategies effectively.

It's also important to be strategic in how you allocate resources within your own team. This involves prioritizing initiatives that align with your overall goals and ensuring that your team has the tools and support they need to succeed. By being mindful of how resources are used, you can maximize their impact and drive greater results.

The Long-Term Impact of Leadership in a Corporate Environment

Leading in a corporate environment comes with its own set of challenges, but it also offers unique opportunities for impact. Leaders who navigate the complexities of corporate life successfully can drive significant change, influence the direction of the organization, and leave a lasting legacy.

For leaders, the long-term impact of their work in a corporate environment is often seen in the culture they help to shape, the innovations they introduce, and the people they mentor and develop. By staying true to their principles, building strong relationships, and effectively managing change, corporate leaders can create a positive and lasting influence on their organization.

Conclusion: Thriving in a Corporate Environment

As we conclude this chapter, it's clear that leading in a corporate environment requires a unique set of skills and strategies. It's about understanding and navigating bureaucracy and politics, balancing short-term pressures with long-term vision, and staying true to your principles in the face of challenges.

In the chapters that follow, we will continue to explore the qualities and practices that are essential for effective leadership. Remember that thriving in a corporate environment is not just about achieving results; it's about leading with integrity, building trust, and creating a positive impact that extends beyond your immediate role.

Leadership in a corporate setting is about more than just managing processes and meeting targets; it's about guiding people, influencing culture, and driving meaningful change within the organization. By embracing the realities of the corporate world and leading with purpose and conviction, you can make a significant difference in your organization and in the lives of the people you lead.

Chapter 11:

The Role of Empathy in Leadership

In the modern workplace, empathy has emerged as one of the most vital qualities for effective leadership. While technical skills and strategic thinking are essential, it is empathy that allows leaders to connect with their teams, understand their needs, and create an environment where people feel valued and motivated. In this chapter, we will explore the role of empathy in leadership, how it can be developed, and the profound impact it can have on both individuals and organizations.

Understanding Empathy in Leadership

Empathy is the ability to understand and share the feelings of others. In leadership, this means being able to put yourself in your team members' shoes, to see things from their perspective, and to respond in a way that acknowledges their emotions and experiences. Empathy goes beyond mere sympathy or compassion; it involves actively engaging with others' feelings and using that understanding to guide your actions and decisions.

Empathy in leadership is not about being soft or letting emotions drive decisions. Instead, it's about making informed decisions that consider the human element. It's recognizing that behind every role, every task, and every performance metric, there are people with their own challenges, aspirations, and emotions.

The Benefits of Empathy in Leadership

Empathetic leadership has far-reaching benefits for both the leader and the organization. One of the most significant advantages is the ability to build stronger relationships with team members. When leaders demonstrate empathy, they build trust and rapport, which in turn fosters loyalty and commitment. Team members are more likely to go the extra mile for a leader who understands and values them as individuals.

Empathy also enhances communication. Leaders who are empathetic are better able to listen to their team members, understand their concerns, and respond in a way that addresses their needs. This leads to more open and honest communication, reduces misunderstandings, and helps to resolve conflicts more effectively.

Moreover, empathy contributes to a positive work environment. When employees feel that their leaders genuinely care about their well-being, they are more likely to feel satisfied and engaged in their work. This not only boosts morale but also leads to higher levels of productivity and creativity. In environments where empathy is practiced, employees are more likely to collaborate, support each other, and contribute to a positive organizational culture.

Cultivating Empathy as a Leader

Empathy is a skill that can be developed and strengthened over time. For leaders who want to cultivate empathy, the first step is to practice active listening. Active listening involves fully focusing on the speaker, avoiding interruptions, and responding thoughtfully. It's about listening to understand, rather than just waiting for your turn to speak. By giving your full attention to others, you can better understand their perspectives and emotions.

Another important aspect of cultivating empathy is being open to feedback. Encourage your team members to share their thoughts and feelings, and be willing to listen with an open mind. This openness not only helps you gain insight into their experiences but also shows that you value their input and are committed to understanding their needs.

Leaders can also develop empathy by seeking out diverse perspectives. Engage with people from different backgrounds, experiences, and roles within the organization. This diversity of thought can help you see situations from various angles and deepen your understanding of the challenges and opportunities that different team members face.

It's also important to practice self-reflection. Take the time to reflect on your own experiences, emotions, and reactions. Consider how your actions and decisions might impact others, and how you would feel in their position. This self-awareness is a key component of empathy, as it helps you recognize your own biases and assumptions, and how they might influence your interactions with others.

"Empathy is the thread that weaves strong leaders and loyal teams together."

Empathy in Decision-Making

Empathy plays a crucial role in decision-making. Leaders who incorporate empathy into their decision-making processes are better equipped to consider the human impact of their choices. This means thinking beyond the immediate outcomes and considering how decisions will affect team members' morale, well-being, and engagement.

For example, when implementing a change that might disrupt the workflow or create uncertainty, an empathetic leader will take the time to communicate the reasons for the change, listen to concerns, and provide support to help team members navigate the transition. This approach not only minimizes resistance but also builds trust and buy-in.

Empathy in decision-making also involves balancing the needs of the organization with the needs of individuals. While leaders must make tough decisions that serve the organization's goals, doing so with empathy ensures that these decisions are made with a consideration of their impact on people. This balance is essential for maintaining trust and fostering a positive work culture.

The Challenges of Empathetic Leadership

While empathy is a powerful tool for leadership, it's not without its challenges. One of the primary challenges is avoiding emotional burnout. Leaders who are highly empathetic may find themselves absorbing the emotions and stress of their team members, which can lead to burnout if not managed carefully. It's important for empathetic leaders to set boundaries, practice self-care, and seek support when needed.

Another challenge is maintaining objectivity. While empathy involves understanding and sharing others' feelings, it's important not to let emotions cloud judgment. Leaders must strike a balance between being empathetic and making decisions that are in the best interest of the organization. This requires emotional intelligence, which includes self-regulation and the ability to manage one's own emotions while understanding others'.

Empathy can also lead to difficult decisions when the needs and desires of individuals conflict with organizational goals. In these situations, leaders must navigate these conflicts carefully, striving to make decisions that are fair, transparent, and considerate of all parties involved.

Empathy and Organizational Culture

Empathy is not just a personal attribute of effective leaders; it's also a critical component of organizational culture. Leaders who prioritize empathy help to create a culture where people feel valued, respected, and supported. This culture of empathy can become a defining characteristic of the organization, influencing how employees interact with each other, how they approach their work, and how they respond to challenges.

An empathetic organizational culture encourages collaboration, innovation, and a sense of community. It fosters an environment where people are willing to take risks, share ideas, and support one another in achieving common goals. This culture can be a powerful driver of organizational success, as it enhances both employee satisfaction and overall performance.

The Long-Term Impact of Empathy in Leadership

The long-term impact of empathy in leadership is profound. Leaders who consistently practice empathy build stronger, more resilient teams. They foster trust, loyalty, and a sense of belonging, which translates into higher levels of engagement and productivity. Empathy also helps to attract and retain top talent, as people are drawn to organizations where they feel understood and valued.

For leaders themselves, practicing empathy leads to personal growth and fulfillment. It deepens their connections with others, enhances their emotional intelligence, and strengthens their ability to lead effectively. Over time, empathetic leaders are more likely to be seen as approachable, trustworthy, and compassionate—qualities that are essential for sustaining long-term success.

Conclusion: Leading with Empathy

As we conclude this chapter, it's clear that empathy is not just a nice-to-have quality in leadership; it's a fundamental component of effective leadership. By cultivating empathy, leaders can build stronger relationships, create a positive work environment, and drive meaningful outcomes for both individuals and the organization.

In the chapters that follow, we will continue to explore the qualities and practices that are essential for effective leadership. Remember that empathy is more than just understanding others' feelings—it's about using that understanding to lead with compassion, make informed decisions, and create a workplace where everyone feels valued and supported.

Leadership is about more than just achieving results; it's about connecting with people, understanding their needs, and guiding them with empathy and care. By leading with empathy, you can create a positive impact that extends far beyond the workplace, shaping a better future for both your team and your organization.

Chapter 12:

Sustaining Your Leadership Journey

Leadership is not a sprint; it's a marathon. Sustaining your leadership journey over the long term requires more than just skill and determination—it requires resilience, self-care, continuous learning, and a deep sense of purpose. In this chapter, we will explore the strategies and practices that can help you maintain your effectiveness as a leader, avoid burnout, and continue to grow both personally and professionally.

The Importance of Resilience

Resilience is the ability to bounce back from setbacks, to adapt to changing circumstances, and to keep moving forward even in the face of challenges. In leadership, resilience is essential because the journey is often filled with obstacles, disappointments, and unexpected turns. Leaders who lack resilience may find themselves overwhelmed by the demands of the role, leading to burnout and a loss of effectiveness.

Building resilience begins with a mindset shift. Instead of viewing challenges as threats, resilient leaders see them as opportunities for growth and learning. This perspective helps them remain positive and proactive, even when things don't go as planned. It also encourages a focus on solutions rather than dwelling on problems.

Another key to resilience is self-awareness. Leaders who are in tune with their own emotions, stress levels, and triggers are better equipped to manage them effectively. This self-awareness allows you to recognize when you need to take a step back, seek support, or adjust your approach to avoid burnout.

The Role of Self-Care in Leadership

Leadership can be demanding, both mentally and physically. To sustain your leadership journey, it's crucial to prioritize self-care. This means taking care of your physical health through regular exercise, a balanced diet, and sufficient sleep. It also means attending to your mental and emotional well-being through activities that help you relax, recharge, and maintain a positive outlook.

Self-care is not a luxury; it's a necessity. Leaders who neglect their own well-being are more likely to experience stress, fatigue, and burnout, which can impair their decision-making, reduce their productivity, and negatively impact their relationships with others.

One important aspect of self-care is setting boundaries. In today's always-connected world, it can be tempting to be available 24/7, but this can lead to burnout. Setting clear boundaries between work and personal life, and sticking to them, helps ensure that you have time to recharge and maintain a healthy work-life balance.

Another aspect of self-care is seeking support when needed. Leadership can be lonely, and it's important to have a support network—whether it's mentors, peers, friends, or family—who can provide advice, encouragement, and a listening ear when you need it.

Continuous Learning and Growth

Effective leaders never stop learning. The world is constantly changing, and leaders who are committed to continuous learning are better equipped to adapt to new challenges and seize new opportunities. Continuous learning also helps to keep your skills sharp, your mind engaged, and your leadership approach fresh.

One way to ensure continuous learning is to seek out new experiences that challenge you and push you out of your comfort zone. This might involve taking on new responsibilities, working on cross-functional projects, or exploring new industries or markets. These experiences not only broaden your knowledge and skills but also help you develop a more versatile and adaptable leadership style.

Formal education and professional development are also important components of continuous learning. Whether through courses, workshops, conferences, or certifications, investing in your own development ensures that you stay up-to-date with the latest trends, tools, and best practices in leadership.

Learning from others is another key aspect of growth. Engage with mentors, coaches, and peers who can offer new perspectives, share their experiences, and provide valuable feedback. These relationships can be incredibly enriching, helping you to see things from different angles and refine your leadership approach.

Staying Connected to Your Purpose

Leadership is not just about achieving goals; it's about staying connected to your deeper purpose—the "why" behind what you do. Purpose is what gives your work meaning and drives you to keep going, even when the journey is difficult.

To sustain your leadership journey, it's important to regularly reconnect with your purpose. Reflect on why you chose to be a leader, what impact you want to have, and what values guide your decisions. This sense of purpose will keep you grounded, motivated, and resilient in the face of challenges.

Purpose also serves as a compass, guiding your decisions and actions. When you're clear about your purpose, you're less likely to be swayed by external pressures or distractions. You're more likely to stay true to your values, make decisions that align with your long-term goals, and lead with integrity.

The Value of Reflection

Reflection is a powerful tool for sustaining your leadership journey. Regularly taking the time to reflect on your experiences, decisions, and outcomes helps you learn from your successes and failures, identify areas for improvement, and stay aligned with your purpose.

Reflection can take many forms, from journaling to meditation to simply taking a walk and thinking about your day. The key is to create space for introspection, where you can step back from the busyness of daily life and consider the bigger picture. This practice not only helps you grow as a leader but also keeps you grounded and focused.

In addition to self-reflection, seek feedback from others. Honest feedback from trusted colleagues, mentors, or team members can provide valuable insights into your leadership style, strengths, and areas for growth. This external perspective is crucial for continuous improvement and helps you stay aware of how you're perceived by others.

Avoiding Burnout

Burnout is a significant risk for leaders, especially those who are deeply committed to their work and their teams. Burnout can manifest as physical and emotional exhaustion, cynicism, and a feeling of reduced accomplishment. If left unchecked, it can lead to a decline in performance, strained relationships, and even health issues.

To avoid burnout, it's important to recognize the signs early and take proactive steps to address them. This might involve adjusting your workload, delegating more responsibilities, or taking time off to recharge. It's also important to maintain a healthy work-life balance and to practice self-compassion—acknowledging that it's okay to take breaks and that you don't have to be perfect.

Organizations also play a role in preventing burnout. As a leader, advocate for a workplace culture that prioritizes well-being, offers support resources, and encourages employees to take care of their mental and physical health. By fostering a supportive environment, you not only help prevent burnout for yourself but also for your team.

The Long-Term Impact of Sustained Leadership

Sustaining your leadership journey has long-term benefits for both you and your organization. Leaders who prioritize resilience, self-care, continuous learning, and connection to purpose are more likely to achieve lasting success, build strong and loyal teams, and create a positive impact on their organization and beyond.

For the leader, a sustained leadership journey leads to personal fulfillment, growth, and a legacy of positive influence. It allows you to continue leading with energy, passion, and purpose, even as you navigate the inevitable ups and downs of leadership.

For the organization, sustained leadership translates into stability, continuity, and ongoing success. Leaders who are committed to their own growth and well-being are better equipped to guide their teams through challenges, drive innovation, and create a thriving workplace culture.

Conclusion: The Journey Continues

As we conclude this chapter and the book, it's clear that leadership is a journey—one that requires dedication, resilience, and a commitment to continuous growth. Sustaining your leadership journey is about more than just achieving short-term success; it's about maintaining your effectiveness, staying true to your values, and leading with purpose over the long term.

Remember that leadership is not a destination but a continuous process of learning, adapting, and growing. By focusing on resilience, self-care, continuous learning, and connection to your purpose, you can sustain your leadership journey and make a lasting impact on those you lead.

Leadership is a marathon, not a sprint. Pace yourself, take care of yourself, and stay connected to what matters most. The journey is long, but it's also incredibly rewarding—filled with opportunities to grow, inspire, and make a difference.

"Leadership is a marathon, not a sprint; pace yourself and stay true to your purpose."

Conclusion: Beyond the Buzzwords

Leadership is a word that gets thrown around a lot. It's discussed in boardrooms, featured in countless books, and touted in seminars and workshops. Yet, for all the talk, true leadership is often misunderstood. Too often, it's reduced to a set of buzzwords—catchy phrases that sound good on paper but rarely translate into real-world results.

As we've explored throughout this book, leadership is about far more than just the language we use to describe it. It's about the actions we take, the principles we live by, and the impact we have on those we lead. It's about moving beyond the buzzwords and focusing on the substance of what it means to lead effectively.

The Gap Between Theory and Practice

One of the central themes of this book has been the gap between leadership theory and practice. Many leadership concepts sound great in theory—ideas like "servant leadership," "transformational leadership," or "visionary leadership." These concepts have their place, and they can provide valuable frameworks for thinking about leadership. But they are only useful if they are put into practice in a way that makes a tangible difference.

Leadership is not just about knowing the right words or following the latest trends. It's about understanding the realities of your environment, the needs of your people, and the unique challenges you face. It's about applying your knowledge in a way that drives real results, whether that's building trust, fostering collaboration, or navigating change.

Real Leadership Requires Action

Leadership is not a passive endeavor; it requires action. It's about making tough decisions, taking responsibility, and leading by example. It's about being there for your team when they need you, communicating with honesty and clarity, and standing firm in your values, even when it's difficult.

Throughout this book, we've explored the qualities that define real leadership—qualities like resilience, empathy, grit, and integrity. These are not just words to be thrown around in meetings; they are principles to be lived out every day. Real leadership requires a commitment to these principles, a willingness to take action, and the courage to lead with authenticity.

The Importance of Authenticity

In a world full of buzzwords, authenticity stands out as one of the most important qualities a leader can possess. Authentic leaders are those who are true to themselves, who lead with integrity, and who inspire trust through their actions. They don't hide behind jargon or clichés; instead, they communicate openly, act consistently, and lead with genuine care for their people.

Authenticity is what separates real leaders from those who merely hold positions of authority. It's what makes people want to follow you, to give their best, and to support your vision. In a time when trust in leadership is more important than ever, authenticity is not just a nice-to-have—it's essential.

Moving Beyond the Buzzwords

As you reflect on the concepts and strategies we've discussed in this book, I encourage you to think about how you can move beyond the buzzwords in your own leadership journey. Ask yourself: How can I apply these principles in a way that makes a real difference? How can I lead with authenticity, integrity, and impact in my day-to-day actions?

Moving beyond the buzzwords means focusing on what really matters—building trust, fostering collaboration, navigating change, and empowering others. It means leading with empathy and resilience, staying true to your values, and committing to continuous growth. It means recognizing that leadership is not about saying the right things but doing the right things.

The Legacy of Real Leadership

At the end of the day, the true measure of your leadership is not in the words you use but in the legacy you leave behind. Real leadership is about the impact you have on the people you lead, the culture you help to create, and the positive changes you drive within your organization. It's about leaving things better than you found them, creating opportunities for others to grow, and leading in a way that inspires others to do the same.

Your leadership journey is unique, and it's up to you to define what success looks like. But as you continue on this journey, remember that the most important thing is to lead with purpose, authenticity, and action. Move beyond the buzzwords, and focus on what really matters. In doing so, you'll not only achieve your own goals but also make a lasting, meaningful impact on those you lead.

Final Thoughts

As we conclude this book, I hope you've found insights, strategies, and inspiration that will help you become the leader you aspire to be. Leadership is a challenging but deeply rewarding journey—one that requires commitment, courage, and a constant willingness to learn and grow.

Remember, leadership is not just about titles or positions; it's about making a difference. It's about leading with integrity, staying true to your values, and moving beyond the buzzwords to focus on real, actionable principles. By doing so, you can lead with impact, inspire others, and create a legacy of positive change.

Thank you for joining me on this journey. Now, it's time to take what you've learned and put it into action. The world needs real leaders—leaders who are willing to move beyond the buzzwords and lead with authenticity and purpose. Will you be one of them?

"Leadership is not defined by the words you use, but by the impact you leave behind."

Leadership Self-Evaluation Worksheet

This worksheet is designed to help you reflect on your current leadership practices, identify areas for growth, and set actionable goals. Based on the content of Authentic Leadership: What Really Works, use this tool to evaluate your leadership status and plan your development journey.

Scoring System:

1 = Needs Improvement: You may be struggling in this area of leadership. Consider focusing on this aspect to develop your skills and effectiveness.

2 = Somewhat Effective: You have some strengths here, but there's room for growth. Identify specific areas where you can improve and take actionable steps.

3 = Adequate: You're doing well, but you might not be reaching your full potential. Look for ways to refine and strengthen your approach.

4 = Strong: You're effective in this area of leadership. Continue building on your strengths and aim for even greater mastery.

5 = Exemplary; You excel in this aspect of leadership. Keep up the great work and consider how you can leverage your strengths to help others grow.

Section 1: The Leadership Myth

Reflection Questions:

What are some common leadership myths that I've believed in the past?

How have these myths influenced my leadership approach?

Self-Assessment:

On a scale of 1-5, how well do I differentiate between leadership theory and practical application in my day-to-day work?

(1 = I often get caught up in theory, 5 = I consistently focus on practical application)

Action Plan:

Identify one leadership myth that you will actively challenge in your current role.

Section 2: Leadership Begins with You

Reflection Questions:

How well do I know my strengths and weaknesses as a leader?

How do I practice self-leadership in my daily life?

Self-Assessment:

On a scale of 1-5, how would I rate my self-awareness as a leader?

(1 = Low awareness, 5 = Highly self-aware)

Action Plan:

Set a goal for improving one area of self-leadership over the next month.

Section 3: The Power of Influence Over Authority

Reflection Questions:

How do I currently influence others? Do I rely more on authority or on building trust and relationships?

What can I do to increase my influence without relying on positional power?

Self-Assessment:

On a scale of 1-5, how effectively do I lead through influence rather than authority?

(1 = I often rely on authority, 5 = I primarily lead through influence)

Action Plan:

Identify one relationship you will work on strengthening through influence rather than authority.

Section 4: Embracing Failure and Learning from It

Reflection Questions:

What recent failures have I experienced, and what did I learn from them?

How do I respond to failure within my team?

Self-Assessment:

On a scale of 1-5, how well do I embrace and learn from failure?

(1 = I struggle with failure, 5 = I see failure as an opportunity for growth)

Action Plan:

Write down a specific failure you will analyze to extract key learnings and apply them going forward.

Section 5: The Importance of Grit and Persistence

Reflection Questions:

When faced with challenges, how persistent am I in pursuing my goals?

How do I model grit and persistence for my team?

Self-Assessment:

On a scale of 1-5, how would I rate my persistence in leadership?

(1 = I give up easily, 5 = I am highly persistent)

Action Plan:

Identify one challenging goal that requires persistence and commit to seeing it through.

Section 6: Authentic Communication

Reflection Questions:

How do I ensure that my communication is clear, honest, and authentic?

What barriers might exist in my communication with my team?

Self-Assessment:

On a scale of 1-5, how authentic is my communication with others?

(1 = I often hold back, 5 = I consistently communicate openly and honestly)

Action Plan:

Set a goal for improving authenticity in one key area of your communication.

Section 7: Leading Through Change

Reflection Questions:

How do I typically respond to change, both personally and as a leader?

What strategies do I use to help my team navigate change?

Self-Assessment:

On a scale of 1-5, how effectively do I lead my team through change?

(1 = I struggle with change, 5 = I excel at managing change)

Action Plan:

Identify an upcoming change and plan how you will lead your team through it.

Section 8: Building and Sustaining Trust

Reflection Questions:

How have I built trust with my team members?

What actions could potentially erode trust in my leadership?

Self-Assessment:

On a scale of 1-5, how strong is the trust between me and my team?

(1 = Low trust, 5 = High trust)

Action Plan:

Choose one trust-building action you will implement this week.

Section 9: The Art of Delegation

Reflection Questions:

How comfortable am I with delegating tasks to others?

What impact does my delegation style have on my team's development?

Self-Assessment:

On a scale of 1-5, how effectively do I delegate tasks?

(1 = I struggle to delegate, 5 = I delegate effectively and regularly)

Action Plan:

Select one task to delegate this week and plan how you will do it.

Section 10: The Realities of Leading in a Corporate Environment

Reflection Questions:

What challenges do I face in navigating the corporate environment?

How do I balance strategy with integrity in my leadership?

Self-Assessment:

On a scale of 1-5, how well do I navigate corporate challenges?

(1 = I struggle with corporate challenges, 5 = I manage them effectively)

Action Plan:

Identify one corporate challenge and plan how you will address it with integrity.

Section 11: The Role of Empathy in Leadership

Reflection Questions:

How do I demonstrate empathy in my interactions with my team?

In what situations might I need to improve my empathy?

Self-Assessment:

On a scale of 1-5, how empathetic am I as a leader?

(1 = I struggle with empathy, 5 = I consistently lead with empathy)

Action Plan:

Practice active listening in your next team interaction and note the difference it makes.

Section 12: Sustaining Your Leadership Journey

Reflection Questions:

What practices do I have in place to sustain my leadership over the long term?

How do I stay connected to my purpose and avoid burnout?

Self-Assessment:

On a scale of 1-5, how well do I sustain my leadership journey?

(1 = I often feel burned out, 5 = I have strong, sustainable practices in place)

Action Plan:

Set a goal to implement one self-care practice that will help sustain your leadership journey.

Conclusion: Beyond the Buzzwords

Reflection Questions:

How do I ensure that my leadership is genuine and impactful, beyond the buzzwords?

What actions will I take to lead with authenticity and purpose?

Self-Assessment:

On a scale of 1-5, how well do I lead beyond the buzzwords?

(1 = I often fall into superficial practices, 5 = I consistently focus on real impact)

Action Plan:

Commit to one action that moves you beyond the buzzwords and towards authentic leadership.

Total Score Range:

45-55: Exceptional Leader

You demonstrate strong leadership qualities across the board. Your team likely benefits greatly from your influence, and you are well on your way to mastering the art of leadership. Keep challenging yourself to maintain and further develop these skills.

35-44: Solid Leader

You have a firm grasp on leadership and are effective in most areas. There may be one or two areas where you could improve, but overall, you're doing well. Identify the areas where you scored lower and focus on refining those skills to elevate your leadership even further.

25-34: Developing Leader

You have some strengths, but there are also several areas where you could grow. This is a great opportunity to focus on specific aspects of your leadership style. Use this evaluation to set concrete goals for improvement and seek out resources or mentorship to help you along the way.

15-24: Emerging Leader

You're in the early stages of developing your leadership abilities. There's significant room for growth, and it's important to actively work on building your skills. Focus on one or two key areas to start with, and gradually work your way up. Consider seeking feedback from peers or mentors to guide your development.

Below 15: Leadership in Progress

You're just beginning your leadership journey, and there's much to learn. Don't be discouraged; everyone starts somewhere. The key is to remain committed to improving and to seek out opportunities for growth. Start with the basics and build a strong foundation of leadership skills over time.

Next Steps:

Reflect on Your Scores: Identify areas where you scored lower and think about why that might be.

Set Specific Goals: Choose one or two areas to focus on improving in the coming weeks or months.

Seek Support: Whether it's through further reading, seminars, or mentorship, find resources to help you strengthen your leadership abilities.

Re-Evaluate: Periodically revisit this worksheet to see how you've progressed and to set new goals.

Jared Scott has spent years immersed in the world of leadership development, devouring countless books, seminars, and workshops on the subject. But after witnessing the persistent gap between leadership theory and the realities of the workplace, He became disillusioned with the empty promises of traditional leadership wisdom. Frustrated by the failure of leadership concepts to deliver real, tangible results, Jared set out to write a book that speaks to the everyday challenges faced by regular people—those who don't see themselves in the glossy leadership profiles of executives and VPs.

www.ingramcontent.com/pod-product-compliance
Lightning Source LLC
Chambersburg PA
CBHW071746240526
45471CB00022B/585